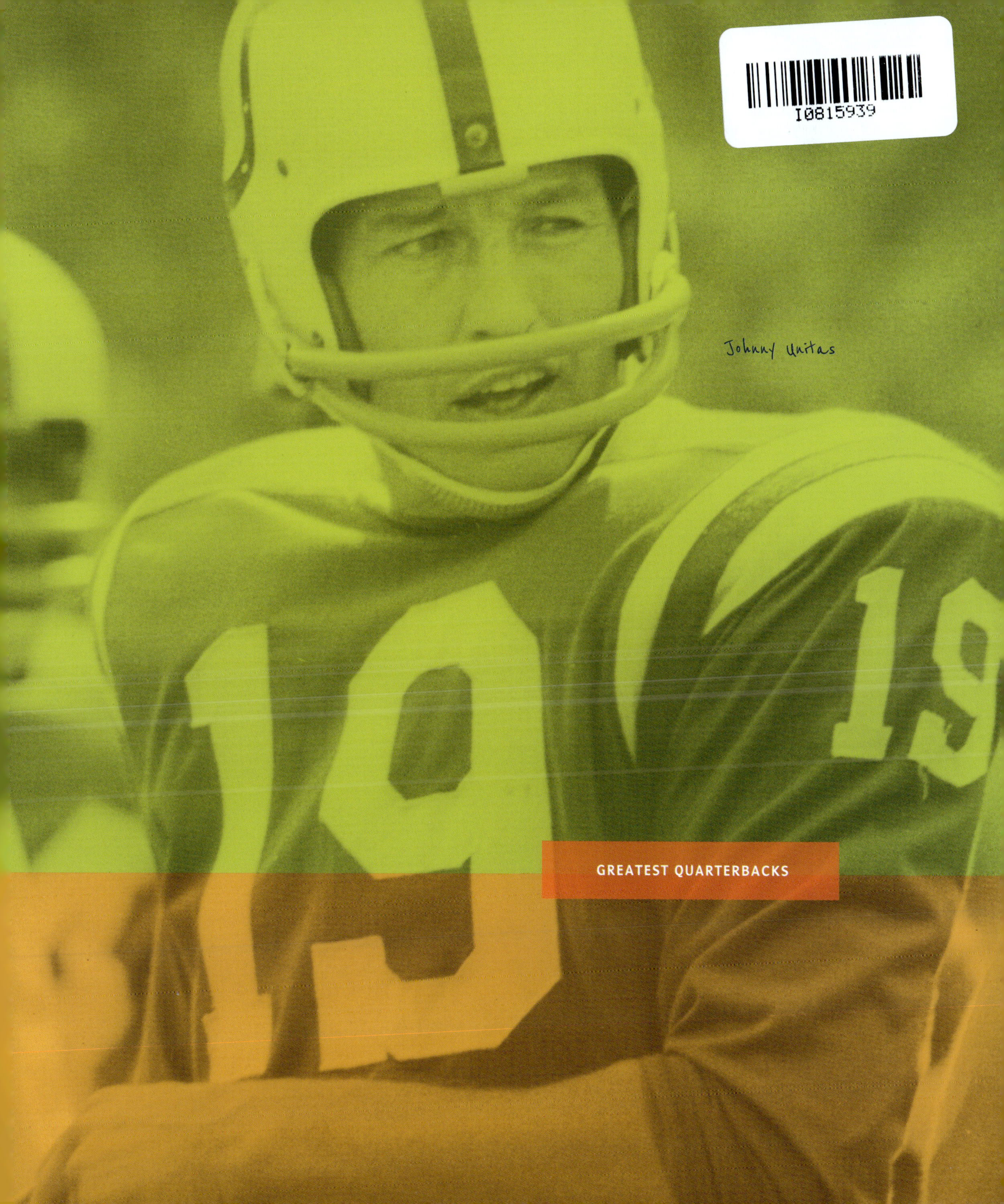
I0815939
Johnny Unitas
GREATEST QUARTERBACKS

Peyton Manning

NFL HALL OF FAMERS

GREATEST QUARTERBACKS

JOE TISCHLER

Otto Graham

CREATIVE EDUCATION / CREATIVE PAPERBACKS

Published by Creative Education and Creative Paperbacks
P.O. Box 227, Mankato, Minnesota 56002
Creative Education and Creative Paperbacks
are imprints of The Creative Company
www.thecreativecompany.us

Design and production by Blue Design (www.bluedes.com)
Art direction by Rita Marshall

Images by Getty Images/Andy Hayt, 29, Bill Eppridge/Time Life Pictures, 7, Focus On Sport, 6, 7, 15, 17, 19, George Gojkovich, 22, Gregory Shamus, 7, Jeff Gross, 30, KARL MONDON/MediaNews Group/Bay Area News, 2, Kidwiler Collection, 7, 18, Michael Zagaris, 6, Mike Powell, 26, NFL/Pro Football Hall Of Fame, 6, Otto Greule Jr, 21, Popperfoto, 25, RHONA WISE, cover, 4–5, 32, Rob Brown, 9, TIMOTHY A. CLARY, 6; Wikimedia Commons/Gonzo fan2007, cover (background), Harris & Ewing, 11, Malcolm W. Emmons, 1, Mass Communication Specialist 1st Class Jennifer A. Villalovos, USN, 28, public domain, 3, 12, 14, Tenschert Photo Co Washington, D.C., 10

Library of Congress Cataloging-in-Publication Data
Names: Tischler, Joe, author.
Title: Greatest quarterbacks / Joe Tischler.
Description: Mankato, Minnesota : Creative Education and Creative Paperbacks, [2026] | Series: Creative sports: NFL hall of famers | Includes index. | Audience: Ages 8–12 | Audience: Grades 4–6 | Summary: "Photo-driven and stat-filled, this middle-grade NFL title showcases 11 of pro football's greatest quarterbacks enshrined in the Hall of Fame, from Sammy Baugh and Joe Montana to Brett Favre and Peyton Manning"— Provided by publisher.
Identifiers: LCCN 2024048105 (print) | LCCN 2024048106 (ebook) | ISBN 9798889896166 (library binding) | ISBN 9781682777824 (paperback) | ISBN 9798889896968 (ebook)
Subjects: LCSH: Quarterbacks (Football)—United States—Biography—Juvenile literature. | Football—United States—Juvenile literature. | National Football League—Juvenile literature.
Classification: LCC GV939.A1 T57 2026 (print) | LCC GV939.A1 (ebook) | DDC 796.332092/2 [B]—dc23/eng/20231120
LC record available at https://lccn.loc.gov/2024048105
LC ebook record available at https://lccn.loc.gov/2024048106

Printed in India

Dan Marino

60

MOSS
81

TAYLOR
56

42
42

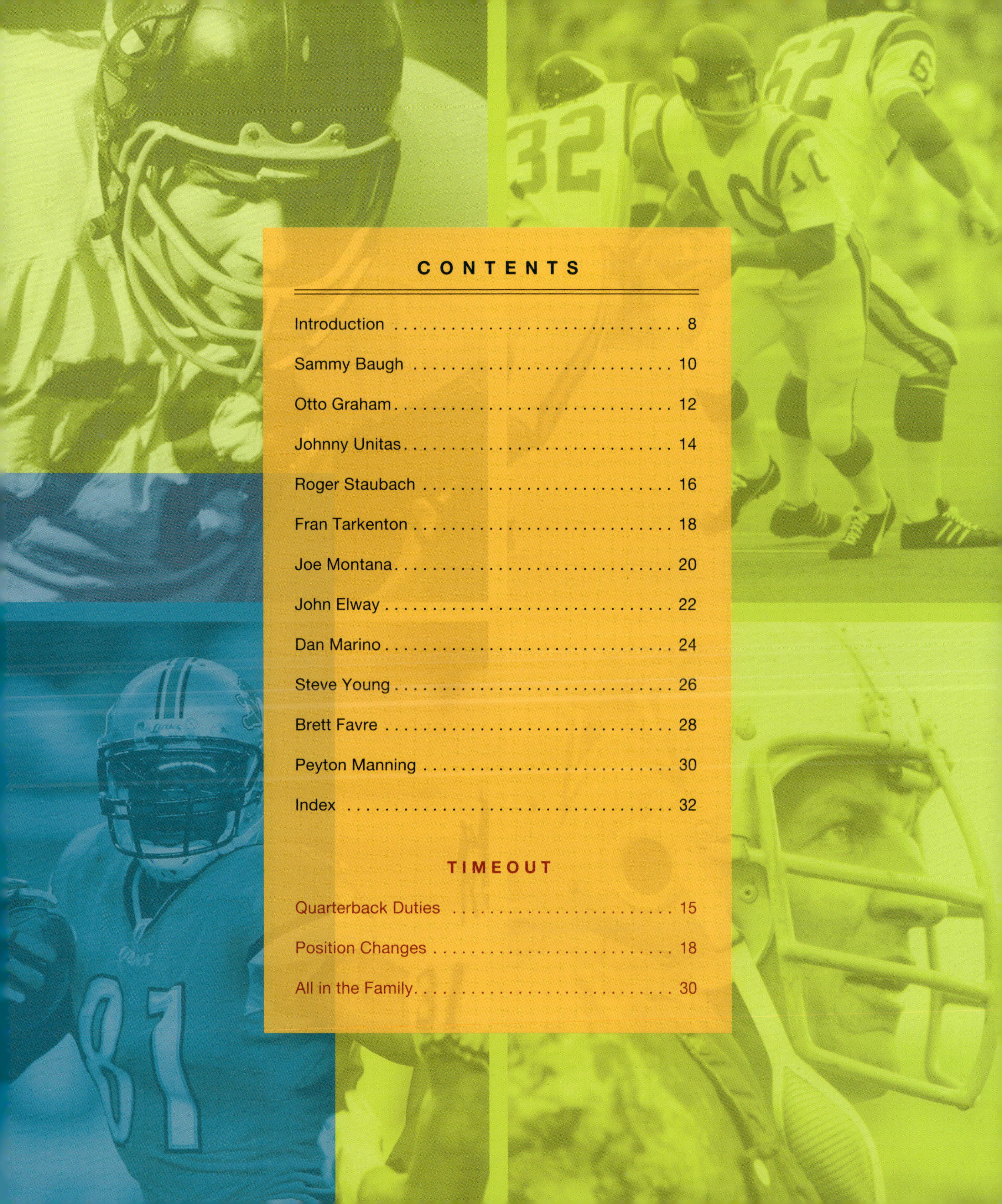

CONTENTS

TIMEOUT

INTRODUCTION

Just 39 seconds remain in Super Bowl XXIII (23). The San Francisco 49ers have the ball on the Cincinnati Bengals' 10-yard line. They trail 16–13. At the snap, 49ers quarterback Joe Montana drops back to pass. He throws and hits John Taylor in the end zone. Touchdown 49ers! It's the third Super Bowl win for Montana.

Football quarterbacks are some of the most important players in all sports. They combine a strong throwing arm with quick decision-making skills and mental focus. They're leaders. All quarterbacks who play for the National Football League (NFL) are at the top of their game. But only a handful can be called Hall of Famers.

The Pro Football Hall of Fame honors 378 past players, coaches, and sport contributors. Of those, just over 30 are quarterbacks. This book highlights 11 Hall of Fame quarterbacks whose careers reached above and beyond. This list isn't a ranking. Players are ordered by the year they were enshrined.

Joe Montana

SAMMY BAUGH (1914–2008)
QUARTERBACK/SAFETY/PUNTER
WASHINGTON REDSKINS SEASONS: 1937–52
HALL OF FAME CLASS: 1963
AWARDS/HONORS: MEMBER OF NFL 75TH/100TH ANNIVERSARY TEAMS, 6X PRO BOWL, 8X ALL-PRO (4X FIRST TEAM), 1940S NFL ALL-DECADE TEAM, 2X NFL CHAMPION

SAMMY BAUGH

One of the greatest all-around athletes in NFL history was Sammy Baugh. He was a star on defense and a star punter. Most of all, he was an amazing quarterback. Baugh was one of the first pure passers of the NFL. In his first season, in 1937, "Slingin Sammy" led the league in pass completions and yardage. He was the only quarterback to throw for more than 1,000 yards that season. He led Washington to an upset win over the Chicago Bears in the NFL Championship Game. Baugh threw for 335 yards and 3 touchdowns. The 335 passing yards remained an NFL rookie record until 2012. In 1942, Baugh and the Redskins defeated the Bears again in the NFL championship.

Baugh had one of the best individual seasons in 1943. As a quarterback, he was second in the league with 1,754 passing yards. As a safety, he led the league with 11 interceptions. The NFL season was only 10 games long in 1943. As a punter, he averaged nearly 46 yards per punt to lead the league. He even had an 81-yard punt. Four times in his career, Baugh led the league in passing yards. Five times he led in punt average. He secured 31 interceptions over his career. He stopped playing defense following the 1945 season.

By the time he retired in 1952, Baugh had set 13 NFL records. In 1963, he was part of the first Pro Football Hall of Fame class.

60

OTTO GRAHAM

OTTO GRAHAM (1921–2003)
QUARTERBACK
CLEVELAND BROWNS SEASONS: 1946–55
HALL OF FAME CLASS: 1965
AWARDS/HONORS: MEMBER OF NFL 75TH/100TH ANNIVERSARY TEAMS, 5X PRO BOWL, 9X ALL-PRO (7X FIRST TEAM), 1950S NFL ALL-DECADE TEAM, 3X NFL MOST VALUABLE PLAYER, 2X AAFC MOST VALUABLE PLAYER, 3X NFL CHAMPION, 4X AAFC CHAMPION

Before the Super Bowl era, Otto Graham was professional football's first biggest winner. He played 10 seasons. In each one, he led the Cleveland Browns to a league championship game. Seven times, he won. Graham's football career began in 1946. The Browns were part of the All-America Football Conference (AAFC). Graham quarterbacked the Browns to a league title that year. He did so again the following three years. Cleveland moved to the NFL in 1950. NFL teams did not think much of the Browns and their top spot in the "lesser" league of the AAFC. Graham proved the critics wrong. The Browns won the NFL championship in their first season in the league. Graham threw four touchdown passes in the title game.

In Graham's 10 seasons, he led the AAFC or NFL in passing yardage 5 times. Five times he led in passer rating. Three times he led in touchdown passes. With Graham, the Browns had an astounding 105–17–4 record. Graham won NFL championships his final two seasons, in 1954 and 1955. His final career game, he ran for two touchdowns and passed for two more.

Before his pro football career, Graham played pro basketball with the Rochester Royals of the National Basketball League (NBL). He had averaged more than five points a game. Rochester won the NBL title. So, make that 11 pro seasons for Graham. Eight championships.

JOHNNY UNITAS

JOHNNY UNITAS (1933–2002)
QUARTERBACK
BALTIMORE COLTS SEASONS: 1956–72; SAN DIEGO CHARGERS SEASON: 1973
HALL OF FAME CLASS: 1979
AWARDS/HONORS: MEMBER OF NFL 50TH/75TH/100TH ANNIVERSARY TEAMS, 10X PRO BOWL, 8X ALL-PRO (5X FIRST TEAM), 1960S NFL ALL-DECADE TEAM, NFL MAN OF THE YEAR, 3X NFL MOST VALUABLE PLAYER, SUPER BOWL CHAMPION, 2X NFL CHAMPION

Johnny Unitas was a man who refused to quit. He waited until the ninth round to be selected in the 1955 NFL Draft by the Pittsburgh Steelers. Pittsburgh released him before the season began. He spent the 1955 season playing semi-pro football for $6 a game. The Baltimore Colts gave Unitas a tryout before the 1956 season. This time, he made the team. He made his first start at quarterback during the season. He became the full-time starter in 1957.

Unitas became a star in 1958. The Colts reached the NFL Championship Game. They trailed the New York Giants 17–14 late in the game. Unitas completed pass after pass down the field to set up a game-tying field goal. It forced the first overtime game in NFL history. In overtime, Unitas led the Colts 80 yards to the game-winning touchdown. The game was called the "Greatest Game Ever Played." Unitas and the Colts won the title again the following season over the Giants. Unitas won his first NFL Most Valuable Player (MVP) award in 1959. In 1960, he became the first quarterback in NFL history to throw for 3,000 yards in a season. Four times he led the league in passing yards. Two more times he earned NFL MVP honors (1964, 1967).

Unitas became the first quarterback to pass for more than 40,000 career yards. He threw 290 career touchdown passes. He threw at least 1 touchdown pass in 47 consecutive games. That was a record that lasted more than 50 years.

QUARTERBACK DUTIES

If a team has an elite quarterback, it will win a lot of games. Quarterbacks are the leaders of the offense. They call the plays in the huddle. They touch the ball on just about every play. Quarterbacks line up directly under the center, who hikes the ball. They may also line up in shotgun formation, usually a few yards behind the center. Quarterbacks pass the ball to open receivers. They scramble to avoid the oncoming defensive rush. Sometimes, they just hand off the ball to the running back.

ROGER STAUBACH

ROGER STAUBACH (1942–)
QUARTERBACK
DALLAS COWBOYS SEASONS: 1969–79
HALL OF FAME CLASS: 1985
AWARDS/HONORS: MEMBER OF NFL 100TH ANNIVERSARY TEAM, 6X PRO BOWL, ALL-PRO, 1970S NFL ALL-DECADE TEAM, NFL MAN OF THE YEAR, 2X SUPER BOWL CHAMPION, SUPER BOWL MVP

Roger Staubach did not take the usual path to NFL stardom. He certainly had the qualifications coming out of college. In 1963, while playing for the U.S. Naval Academy, Staubach won the Heisman Trophy. The award is given to the season's best college football player. Even so, Staubach was not taken high in the 1964 NFL Draft. Graduates of the U.S. Naval Academy had four years of military commitment before they could play professionally. So, Staubach was not taken until the 10th round.

Staubach finally entered the NFL in 1969 with the Dallas Cowboys. He started only four games at quarterback over his first two seasons. He was named full-time starter in 1971. The Cowboys rode his scrambling ability and high passer rating to Super Bowl VI (6). Staubach earned Super Bowl MVP honors as the Cowboys won their first title. That was just the beginning of the Cowboys' winning streak. Staubach was the team's full-time starting quarterback for eight seasons. Six times the Cowboys reached the National Football Conference (NFC) Championship Game. Four times they reached the Super Bowl. Two times they were champions.

Staubach was given many nicknames during his career. Among them were "Captain America," "Captain Comeback," and "Roger the Dodger." He was largely credited with the "Hail Mary" pass. In a 1975 NFC Divisional Playoff game against the Minnesota Vikings, Staubach threw a 50-yard touchdown pass in the closing seconds for the win. He noted that he said a "Hail Mary" prayer when the ball was thrown.

Fran Tarkenton

POSITION CHANGES

Rules have changed over time to protect the quarterback. Defensive players were once allowed to hit the quarterback from head to toe. Today, a defender is not allowed to hit the quarterback in the head or tackle him below the knees. Too many quarterbacks were getting injured this way. In 2008, New England Patriots quarterback Tom Brady hurt his knee in the season opener on a low hit. He did not play the rest of the season. The following season, a new rule penalized defenders for this type of hit.

FRAN TARKENTON (1940–)
QUARTERBACK
MINNESOTA VIKINGS SEASONS: 1961–66, 1972–78; NEW YORK GIANTS SEASONS: 1967–71
HALL OF FAME CLASS: 1986
AWARDS/HONORS: 9X PRO BOWL, 2X ALL-PRO (1X FIRST TEAM), NFL MOST VALUABLE PLAYER, NFL OFFENSIVE PLAYER OF THE YEAR

FRAN TARKENTON

Nicknamed "The Scrambler," Fran Tarkenton used his ability to run from defenders to become one of football's greatest passers. Tarkenton was a master at keeping one eye on oncoming linemen and another eye downfield, looking for an open receiver. He rushed for more than 3,600 yards in his career. He also threw for just over 47,000 yards and more than 340 touchdowns. He held every major passing record by the time he retired after the 1978 season.

Tarkenton started his career with the expansion Minnesota Vikings in 1961. He played with them until 1967. In his (and the franchise's) first-ever game, he threw for four touchdowns. He also ran for a fifth in the upset win over the Chicago Bears. After a five-year stint with the New York Giants, Tarkenton went back to the Vikings in 1972. He led Minnesota to three Super Bowl appearances over a four-year period. But the team lost each time. Tarkenton's best season was 1975. The Vikings won their first 10 games of the season and finished with a 12–2 record. Tarkenton led the league with 25 touchdown passes. He was named NFL Most Valuable Player and NFL Offensive Player of the Year. But the Vikings were victims of the "Hail Mary" pass in the NFC Divisional Playoffs.

In his second term with Minnesota, Tarkenton led the Vikings to six division titles in seven years. Overall, he was selected to play in nine Pro Bowls.

JOE MONTANA

JOE MONTANA (1956–)
QUARTERBACK
SAN FRANCISCO 49ERS SEASONS: 1979–92; KANSAS CITY CHIEFS SEASONS: 1993–94
HALL OF FAME CLASS: 2000
AWARDS/HONORS: MEMBER OF NFL 75TH/100TH ANNIVERSARY TEAMS, 8X PRO BOWL, 5X ALL-PRO (3X FIRST TEAM), 1980S NFL ALL-DECADE TEAM, 2X NFL MOST VALUABLE PLAYER, NFL OFFENSIVE PLAYER OF THE YEAR, 4X SUPER BOWL CHAMPION, 3X SUPER BOWL MVP

The San Francisco 49ers were the team of the 1980s. They won four Super Bowl championships in the decade. The starting quarterback for each one was Joe Montana. He was a third-round selection of the 49ers in the 1979 NFL Draft. San Francisco won just two games his first season. Montana became the full-time starting quarterback in 1981. He guided the team to 13 wins and its first Super Bowl title. "Joe Cool" earned his nickname for keeping calm in the biggest of moments. That "coolness" started in college, when Montana led the University of Notre Dame to a national championship. And it continued in the NFL. Montana is one of only two quarterbacks to win both a Super Bowl and a college football national title.

Montana was the first player to win three Super Bowl MVP awards. In 4 Super Bowl games, he threw 11 touchdown passes. More impressively, he did not throw a single interception. He threw five touchdown passes in his final Super Bowl appearance, a 55–10 win over the Denver Broncos in Super Bowl XXIV (24). The 45-point win is the largest margin of victory in a Super Bowl.

Montana was just as great in the regular season. He earned back-to-back NFL MVP honors in 1989 and 1990. He was selected to the Pro Bowl eight times. Three times he earned First Team All-Pro honors.

49ERS
16

JOHN ELWAY

JOHN ELWAY (1960–)
QUARTERBACK
DENVER BRONCOS SEASONS: 1983–98
HALL OF FAME CLASS: 2004
AWARDS/HONORS: MEMBER OF NFL 100TH ANNIVERSARY TEAM, 9X PRO BOWL, 3X ALL-PRO, 1990S NFL ALL-DECADE TEAM, NFL MAN OF THE YEAR, NFL MOST VALUABLE PLAYER, 2X SUPER BOWL CHAMPION, SUPER BOWL MVP

John Elway had the perfect end to a Hall of Fame career. In his 16th and final season, he guided the Denver Broncos to a 14–2 record. Denver won its second straight Super Bowl championship. And Elway was named the MVP of Super Bowl XXXIII (33) in the final game of his career. Elway is the only player in history to be named Super Bowl MVP in his final career game.

Elway was the number one pick of the 1983 NFL Draft. The Baltimore Colts selected him. They then traded him to Denver. It was a trade that forever changed the Denver franchise. By his fourth season, Elway had led Denver to the Super Bowl. In the 1986 American Football Conference (AFC) Championship Game, Elway led "The Drive." It was a 98-yard touchdown drive that tied the game late against the Cleveland Browns. Elway was well known for his comebacks. He holds the NFL record with 47 fourth-quarter game-winning or game-tying drives in the regular and postseason.

It would take 15 years for Elway and Denver to win that elusive Super Bowl title. After failing in his first three Super Bowl tries, Elway led the team to victory. Denver beat the Green Bay Packers 31–24 in Super Bowl XXXII (32). Elway was the first quarterback to start five Super Bowls. At the time he retired, he had recorded the most victories (149) by a starting quarterback in NFL history.

DAN MARINO

DAN MARINO (1961–)
QUARTERBACK
MIAMI DOLPHINS SEASONS: 1983–99
HALL OF FAME CLASS: 2004
AWARDS/HONORS: MEMBER OF NFL 100TH ANNIVERSARY TEAM, 9X PRO BOWL, 6X ALL-PRO (3X FIRST TEAM), NFL MAN OF THE YEAR, NFL MOST VALUABLE PLAYER, NFL OFFENSIVE PLAYER OF THE YEAR

Another quarterback from the 1983 NFL Draft to play his entire NFL career with one team was Dan Marino. While John Elway was the first player selected in that draft, Marino waited until the 27th selection to hear his name called. The Miami Dolphins got him. Marino made a huge impact right away. In 1984, just his second season in the league, Marino became the first quarterback in history to throw for more than 5,000 yards in a season. He shattered a then-NFL record with 48 touchdown passes. The previous record for a season was 36. The Dolphins won 14 games in 1984 and reached the Super Bowl. But they lost to the San Francisco 49ers. It would turn out to be the only Super Bowl appearance of Marino's career. Marino is considered one of the greatest players to never win a Super Bowl.

Despite the Super Bowl loss, Marino continued to put up stellar numbers. Four more times he led the NFL in passing yards in a season. Two more times he led the league in touchdown passes. At his retirement, Marino held the NFL record for career touchdown passes (420) and career passing yards (61,361).

The Dolphins reached the playoffs in 10 of Marino's 17 seasons. He was selected to play in nine Pro Bowls. Six times he was named First or Second Team All-Pro. He is the first quarterback in NFL history to have at least six 4,000-yard passing seasons.

STEVE YOUNG

STEVE YOUNG (1961–)
QUARTERBACK
TAMPA BAY BUCCANEERS SEASONS: 1985–86; SAN FRANCISCO 49ERS SEASONS: 1987–99
HALL OF FAME CLASS: 2005
AWARDS/HONORS: 7X PRO BOWL, 6X ALL-PRO (3X FIRST TEAM), 2X NFL MOST VALUABLE PLAYER, NFL OFFENSIVE PLAYER OF THE YEAR, 3X SUPER BOWL CHAMPION, SUPER BOWL MVP

Steve Young had an unusual path to becoming a star quarterback. He began his professional career playing in a different league, the United States Football League (USFL). Young played two seasons with the Los Angeles Express. When the USFL folded, Young moved to the NFL. He began his NFL career with the Tampa Bay Buccaneers. He started 19 games over 2 seasons. Tampa Bay won only four games during that time. Young was traded to the San Francisco 49ers. There, he was backup to future hall of famer Joe Montana for four seasons. Montana was hurt in 1991, allowing Young to be the starter.

With Young, the 49ers won 14 games in 1992. Young led the NFL in several categories, including passer rating and touchdown passes. He was named NFL MVP. He led the NFL in touchdown passes the following two seasons as well. He repeated as NFL MVP in 1994. The 49ers won 13 games and reached Super Bowl XXIX (29). San Francisco destroyed the San Diego Chargers, 49–26. Young set a Super Bowl record with six touchdown passes. He was named Super Bowl MVP.

Young was one of the most accurate passers in NFL history. He led the league in completion percentage five times. Four times he led the league in touchdown passes. Young is one of only two left-handed quarterbacks in the Hall of Fame. The other is Ken Stabler, who played from 1970 to 1984.

BRETT FAVRE

BRETT FAVRE (1969–)
QUARTERBACK
ATLANTA FALCONS SEASON: 1991; GREEN BAY PACKERS SEASONS: 1992–2007; NEW YORK JETS SEASON: 2008; MINNESOTA VIKINGS SEASONS: 2009–10
HALL OF FAME CLASS: 2016
AWARDS/HONORS: MEMBER OF NFL 100TH ANNIVERSARY TEAM, 11X PRO BOWL, 6X ALL-PRO (3X FIRST TEAM), 1990S NFL ALL-DECADE TEAM, 3X NFL MOST VALUABLE PLAYER, NFL OFFENSIVE PLAYER OF THE YEAR, SUPER BOWL CHAMPION

Brett Favre did not have the best start to his Hall of Fame career. He was selected by the Atlanta Falcons in the second round of the 1991 NFL Draft. He threw only four passes in 1991. Two of those four were intercepted. The first was returned for a touchdown. Favre was traded to the Green Bay Packers the following season. In 1992, he came off the bench to lead the Packers to a come-from-behind win. He started the next game. And he started every other game through 13 games of the 2010 season. That NFL-record streak lasted 297 games (321, including playoffs). At his retirement, Favre held every major passing record, including passing yards (71,838) and touchdown passes (508).

Favre led the Packers to the playoffs in his second season in Green Bay. In 1995, he earned the first of three straight NFL Most Valuable Player honors. He is the only player to win three straight MVPs. In 1996, the Packers won 13 games and reached Super Bowl XXXI (31). Favre threw for two touchdowns and ran for another in the team's 35–21 win over the New England Patriots. He led the Packers back to the Super Bowl the following season. But they lost to the Denver Broncos.

Favre ended his career with the New York Jets and the Minnesota Vikings. He had one of his best seasons in 2009 with Minnesota. He had 33 touchdown passes and threw only 7 interceptions.

Peyton Manning

ALL IN THE FAMILY

Archie Manning was selected with the number two pick of the 1971 NFL Draft by the New Orleans Saints. He played 14 seasons but never played for a winning team. His sons, though, won plenty of games. Peyton Manning was the number one pick in the 1998 NFL Draft by the Indianapolis Colts. He won five MVPs and two Super Bowls. His brother, Eli, was the number one pick in the 2004 NFL Draft by the New York Giants. He also won two Super Bowls. Peyton and Eli have remained in the public eye after their pro football retirement. The brothers star in several commercials and are co-hosts of the *ManningCast*, providing live commentary during Monday Night Football games.

PEYTON MANNING

PEYTON MANNING (1976–)
QUARTERBACK
INDIANAPOLIS COLTS SEASONS: 1998–2011; DENVER BRONCOS SEASONS: 2012–15
HALL OF FAME CLASS: 2021
AWARDS/HONORS: MEMBER OF NFL 100TH ANNIVERSARY TEAM, 14X PRO BOWL, 10X ALL-PRO (7X FIRST TEAM), 2000S NFL ALL-DECADE TEAM, NFL MAN OF THE YEAR, 5X NFL MOST VALUABLE PLAYER, 2X NFL OFFENSIVE PLAYER OF THE YEAR, 2X SUPER BOWL CHAMPION, SUPER BOWL MVP

Throughout his 18-year NFL career, Peyton Manning set records. Those records started in his rookie season. The Indianapolis Colts selected Manning with the first overall pick of the 1998 NFL Draft. The team won only three games that year. But Manning set NFL rookie records for passing yards and touchdown passes. His stardom only grew from there. The Colts jumped to 13 wins in 1999. Manning earned the first of his 14 Pro Bowl nods. In 2003, he received the first of his NFL-record five NFL Most Valuable Player awards. The following season, he set a then-NFL record with 49 touchdown passes. He broke that record again in 2013 with 55 while playing for the Denver Broncos. That year, he set an NFL record for passing yards in a season with 5,477.

In Manning's 13 seasons as starting quarterback, the Colts made the playoffs 11 times. Eight times the Colts won their division. Twice the Colts reached the Super Bowl with one championship. Manning was named MVP of Super Bowl XLI (41) following the 2006 season. After missing 2011 with a neck injury, he signed with Denver in 2012. He continued to win there. The Broncos won division titles in all four seasons. The Broncos reached two Super Bowls, including a win in Super Bowl 50.

INDEX